CHARTING PROGRESS

U.S. MILITARY NON-MEDICAL COUNSELING PROGRAMS

Thomas E. Trail, Laurie T. Martin, Lane F. Burgette, Linnea Warren May,
Ammarah Mahmud, Nupur Nanda, Anita Chandra

RAND
CORPORATION

Prepared for the Deputy Assistant Secretary of Defense
for Military Community and Family Policy

Approved for public release; distribution unlimited

This publication describes work done in the RAND National Defense Research Institute
and documented in *An Evaluation of U.S. Military Non-Medical Counseling Programs*, by
Thomas E. Trail, Laurie T. Martin, Lane F. Burgette, Linnea Warren May,
Ammarah Mahmud, Nupur Nanda, and Anita Chandra, RR-1861-OSD, 2017.

For more information on this publication,
visit www.rand.org/t/RR1861z1

Support RAND
Make a tax-deductible charitable contribution at
www.rand.org/giving/contribute

www.rand.org

Contents

Introduction

The Department of Defense (DoD) offers short-term, solution-focused counseling for common personal and family issues that do not warrant medical or behavioral health treatment within the military health system. These counseling services, called *non-medical counseling* within DoD, are typically implemented outside traditional health care settings. They are aimed at addressing a broad array of common problems associated with life in general and military life in particular.

DoD offers non-medical counseling through two complementary programs: the Military and Family Life Counseling (MFLC) program and Military OneSource, both administered by the Office of Deputy Assistant Secretary of Defense for Military Community and Family Policy (ODASD [MC&FP]). Established in 2004, these programs were developed to provide a confidential platform to address daily stressors and to reduce the stigma that is generally associated with military counseling. The MFLC program and Military OneSource are offered at no cost to members of the active and reserve components and their families, for up to 12 sessions per person, per presenting problem.

Evaluation Design and Approach

RAND recently completed an evaluation of non-medical counseling provided through the MFLC program and Military OneSource.[*]

For both the MFLC program and Military OneSource, we conducted two online surveys. The first was completed approximately two to three weeks after a participant's initial counseling session and was designed to capture the participants' retrospective assessments of the severity of their problem, the perceived impact of the problem on their life prior to counseling, and an assessment of their problem's severity and perceived impact shortly after initiating non-medical counseling (i.e., short-term outcomes).

The second survey was completed three months later and asked similar questions, allowing an examination of changes over time in problem severity, stress and anxiety, and effects on work and family life (i.e., long-term outcomes). Because the programs provide short-term, solution-focused non-medical counseling for twelve sessions, three months was considered a reasonable period of time to measure problem resolution. Participants were also asked to provide open-ended responses to two questions assessing the perceived strengths and weaknesses of the MFLC program or Military OneSource program.

Data collection occurred from October 2014–November 2016 for the MFLC program, and April 2015–November 2016 for Military OneSource. Both studies collected data for a full calendar year, at a minimum, to ensure that findings were not driven by any potential seasonal variation in non-medical concerns or service use. A total of 2,585 MFLC program and 2,892 Military OneSource

participants responded to the Wave 1 survey, and 614 MFLC program and 878 Military OneSource participants responded to the Wave 2 survey. Participants in the study were limited to adults aged 18 years or older who received at least one in-person non-medical counseling session of 30 minutes or more in an individual or couples setting. Service members and eligible family members across the Air Force, Army, Marine Corps, Navy, and National Guard participated in the study.

Response rates for both the MFLC program and Military OneSource were low, but not atypical for studies of military service members and their families. The demographic characteristics and problem type for the study participants were generally consistent with the population of individuals seeking services from these programs. Where there were differences between the sample and population characteristics, we adjusted the data to be representative of the population of program users.

The study used a longitudinal design to understand whether individuals participating in non-medical counseling report improvements in important outcomes related to military and family readiness, such as problem severity, stress, and problem interference in their work and daily lives. However, the study did not include a control group that received either no treatment or a different type of treatment; as a result, we cannot draw causal conclusions about the effectiveness of the program. The study was also not designed to evaluate specific therapeutic approaches or training provided by non-medical counselors.

[*] Thomas E. Trail, Laurie T. Martin, Lane F. Burgette, Linnea Warren May, Ammarah Mahmud, Nupur Nanda, and Anita Chandra, *An Evaluation of U.S. Military Non-Medical Counseling Programs*, Santa Monica, CA: RAND Corporation, 2017. www.rand.org/t/RR1861.html

Non-Medical Counseling Through the MFLC Program and Military OneSource: Two Complementary Modalities for Non-Medical Counseling

Both the MFLC program and Military OneSource programs provide non-medical counseling to military service members and their families, but do so through distinct modalities to ensure widespread access to non-medical counseling:

MFLC program

- In-person counseling

- Counselors are located at military installations or visit installations regularly

- Counseling provided at installations or other convenient, confidential location

- Appointments do not require referral

Military OneSource

- Counseling via in-person sessions, phone, online instant messaging, as well as online video calls.

- Counseling is provided by a counselor with an office in the local civilian community

- Referral from Military OneSource consultant required

Because of these differences, this study was not designed or intended to facilitate comparisons across the two programs.

While findings were largely consistent across the MFLC program and Military OneSource, differences in program delivery, study methodology, and the populations each program serves preclude direct comparisons between the two programs. Differences between programs should not be interpreted as evidence of one program's strength over the other.

REASONS TO SEEK NON-MEDICAL COUNSELING

Participants reported using non-medical counseling services for a wide range of concerns. More than two-thirds sought help with family or relationship problems.

PARTICIPANTS COULD CHECK
ALL THAT APPLIED.

◻ MFLC program
◼ Military OneSource

Family or relationship issues

67.8%
73.6%

Stress, anxiety, or emotional problems

55.3%
43.1%

Conflict resolution or anger management

26.1%
20.8%

Other reported problem types include:

- Loss or grief

- Child issues (e.g., academic, behavioral)

- Deployment concerns or support

- Exceptional family member support

- Reintegration concerns or support

- Relocation/permanent change of station concerns or support

- Wounded warrior concerns or support

- Personal financial management

- Employment assistance

- Education assistance (for self or spouse)

- Care for disabled or elderly adult.

SHORT-TERM CHANGES IN PROBLEM SEVERITY

Shortly after counseling, the majority of MFLC program and Military OneSource participants reported a reduction in problem severity.

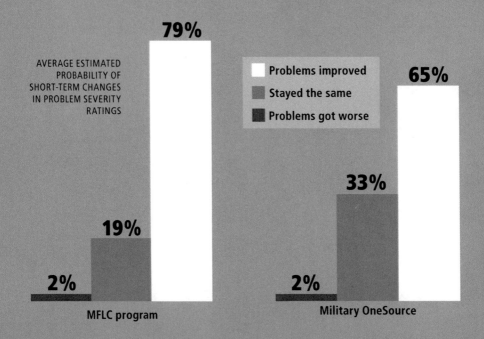

AVERAGE ESTIMATED
PROBABILITY OF
SHORT-TERM CHANGES
IN PROBLEM SEVERITY
RATINGS

- Problems improved
- Stayed the same
- Problems got worse

79%

19%

2%

MFLC program

65%

33%

2%

Military OneSource

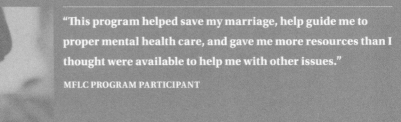

"This program helped save my marriage, help guide me to proper mental health care, and gave me more resources than I thought were available to help me with other issues."

MFLC PROGRAM PARTICIPANT

LONG-TERM CHANGES IN PROBLEM SEVERITY

A reduction in problem severity was maintained or continued to improve over a three-month period after counseling.

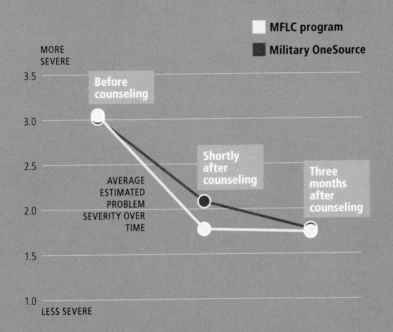

□ MFLC program

■ Military OneSource

MORE SEVERE

3.5

Before counseling

3.0

2.5

Shortly after counseling

Three months after counseling

AVERAGE ESTIMATED PROBLEM SEVERITY OVER TIME

2.0

1.5

1.0

LESS SEVERE

RATINGS WERE MADE ON A FOUR-POINT SCALE, FROM LOW TO VERY SEVERE.

"[Military OneSource] has helped me cope with my husband's deployment, helped us re-connect now that he's home, helped our family dynamic, helped me as an individual. We would be so much worse off without this service. Our provider/counselor is awesome and has helped us gain a stronger marriage and has helped me to be a better spouse."

MILITARY ONESOURCE PARTICIPANT

SHORT-TERM CHANGES IN STRESS AND ANXIETY

More than 70 percent of individuals reported a reduction in the frequency of feeling stressed or anxious after initiating counseling.

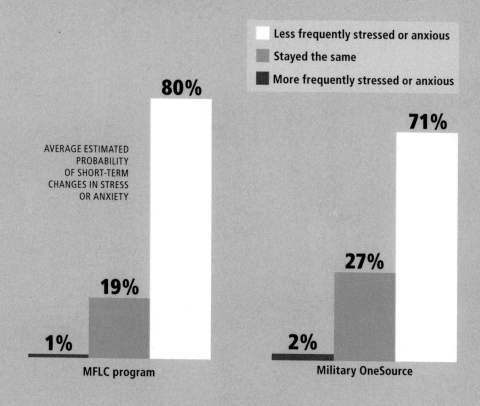

Less frequently stressed or anxious

Stayed the same

More frequently stressed or anxious

AVERAGE ESTIMATED PROBABILITY OF SHORT-TERM CHANGES IN STRESS OR ANXIETY

80%

71%

27%

19%

1%

2%

MFLC program

Military OneSource

"The counseling definitely helps with stresses brought on by the highly demanding military way of life."

MILITARY ONESOURCE PARTICIPANT

LONG-TERM CHANGES IN STRESS AND ANXIETY

Stress or anxiety continued to improve over a three-month period after counseling.

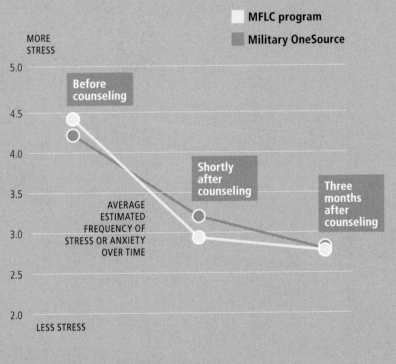

MFLC program

Military OneSource

MORE STRESS

5.0

Before counseling

4.5

4.0

Shortly after counseling

3.5

Three months after counseling

AVERAGE ESTIMATED FREQUENCY OF STRESS OR ANXIETY OVER TIME

3.0

2.5

2.0

LESS STRESS

RATINGS WERE MADE ON A FIVE-POINT SCALE, FROM NEVER TO VERY FREQUENTLY.

"It's really easy to feel a connection with the MFLC .... The MFLC has made the amount of work and personal stress drop drastically. I hope this program never goes away."

MFLC PROGRAM PARTICIPANT

INTERFERENCE WITH WORK

Three months after counseling, around 8 percent of participants reported that their problem frequently or very frequently interfered with their work, compared to about 40 percent before counseling.

AVERAGE ESTIMATED
PROBABILITY OF
FREQUENCY OF
PROBLEM INTERFERENCE
WITH WORK OVER TIME

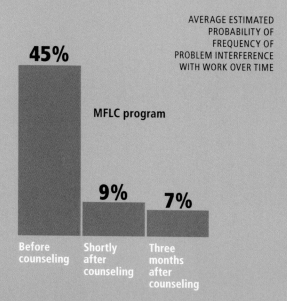

MFLC program

45%

9%

7%

Before counseling

Shortly after counseling

Three months after counseling

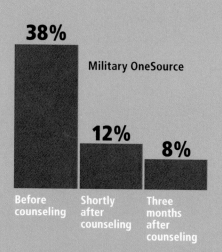

Military OneSource

38%

12%

8%

Before counseling

Shortly after counseling

Three months after counseling

"Having someone on hand who both understa the military/aviation culture and the effects it has on family life immediately causes an atmo sphere of understanding.... This facilitated a very rapid healing process for me and my wife cannot express how instrumental our counsel was in aiding my immediate return to duty."

MFLC PROGRAM PARTICIPANT

INTERFERENCE WITH DAILY ROUTINES
Three months after counseling, around 11 percent of participants reported that their problem frequently or very frequently interfered with their daily routines, compared to about 55 percent before counseling.

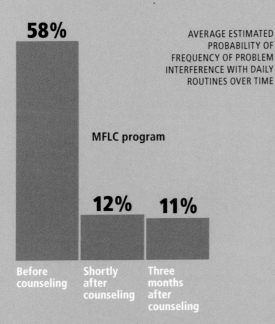

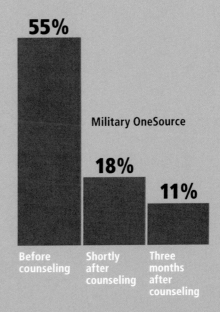

AVERAGE ESTIMATED PROBABILITY OF FREQUENCY OF PROBLEM INTERFERENCE WITH DAILY ROUTINES OVER TIME

58%

MFLC program

12%

11%

Before counseling

Shortly after counseling

Three months after counseling

55%

Military OneSource

18%

11%

Before counseling

Shortly after counseling

Three months after counseling

"I am so profoundly grateful that Military OneSource is available. As a result of these services . . . I feel more fit in both my personal and professional life and only regret that I did not take advantage of them sooner."

MILITARY ONESOURCE PARTICIPANT

SPEED OF CONNECTING TO SERVICES
More than 90 percent of individuals were satisfied with the speed of being connected to a counselor.

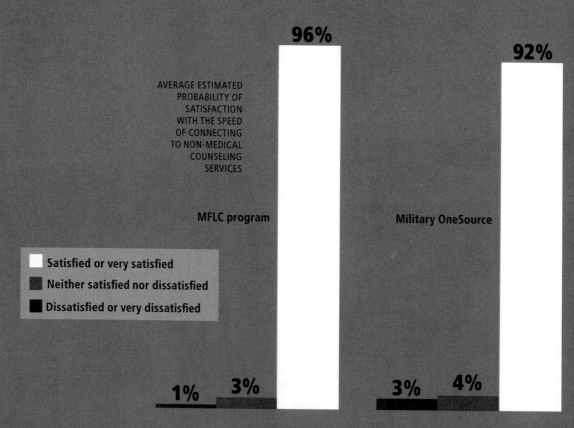

AVERAGE ESTIMATED PROBABILITY OF SATISFACTION WITH THE SPEED OF CONNECTING TO NON-MEDICAL COUNSELING SERVICES

96%

92%

MFLC program

Military OneSource

☐ Satisfied or very satisfied
■ Neither satisfied nor dissatisfied
■ Dissatisfied or very dissatisfied

1% 3%

3% 4%

"Military OneSource was able to find a counselor that specialized in what I was looking for and near me. It would have taken me hours/days to figure it out. I called very late in the evening and was able to speak to someone right away. I got the contact info for a counselor and left a message for them. They called back the next morning even though it was a weekend and [I] was able to get an appointment very quickly."

MILITARY ONESOURCE PARTICIPANT

16

CONFIDENTIALITY OF PERSONAL AND FAMILY INFORMATION

More than 90 percent of individuals were satisfied with the confidentiality of personal and family information held by the program.

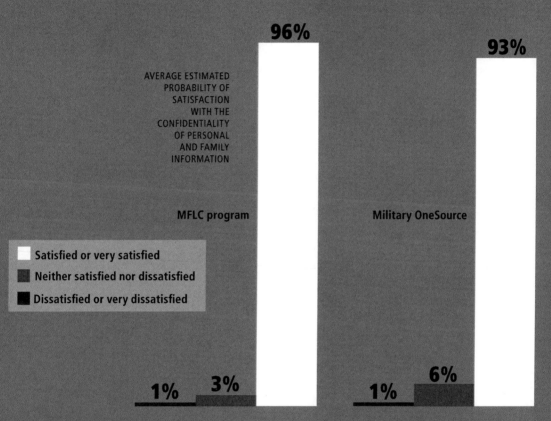

AVERAGE ESTIMATED
PROBABILITY OF
SATISFACTION
WITH THE
CONFIDENTIALITY
OF PERSONAL
AND FAMILY
INFORMATION

MFLC program — 96%, 1%, 3%

Military OneSource — 93%, 1%, 6%

☐ Satisfied or very satisfied
■ Neither satisfied nor dissatisfied
■ Dissatisfied or very dissatisfied

"[A strength of the program is] the fact that MFLC counselors are not plugged into the same healthcare recording systems as medical services which leads me to believe confidentiality is better and makes me feel more comfortable about using the service."

MFLC PROGRAM PARTICIPANT

NECESSARY SERVICES WERE PROVIDED BY COUNSELOR

About 90 percent of participants felt that their counselor provided the services they needed to address their non-medical problems and related concerns.

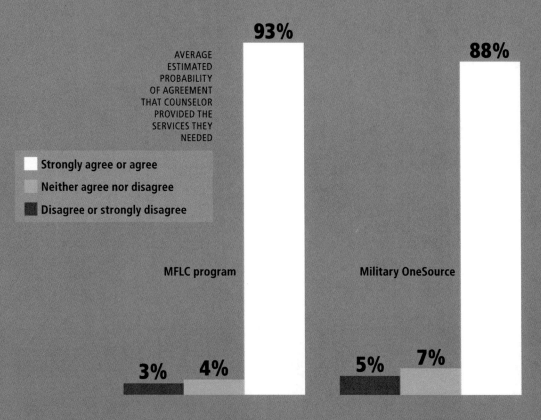

AVERAGE
ESTIMATED
PROBABILITY
OF AGREEMENT
THAT COUNSELOR
PROVIDED THE
SERVICES THEY
NEEDED

Strongly agree or agree

Neither agree nor disagree

Disagree or strongly disagree

93%

88%

MFLC program

Military OneSource

3%   4%

5%   7%

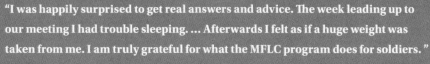

"I was happily surprised to get real answers and advice. The week leading up to our meeting I had trouble sleeping. ... Afterwards I felt as if a huge weight was taken from me. I am truly grateful for what the MFLC program does for soldiers."

MFLC PROGRAM PARTICIPANT

LIKELIHOOD OF FUTURE PROGRAM USE

More than 90 percent of participants reported that they would be likely or highly likely to use non-medical counseling services again if the need arose.

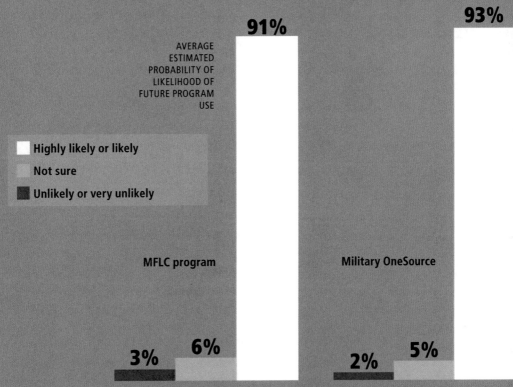

AVERAGE ESTIMATED PROBABILITY OF LIKELIHOOD OF FUTURE PROGRAM USE

- Highly likely or likely
- Not sure
- Unlikely or very unlikely

91%

93%

MFLC program

Military OneSource

3% **6%**

2% **5%**

"My counselor knew me and counseled me in a way I responded well to. Appointments were flexible and encouraged me to come back. I would definitely use an MFLC again when I needed support."

MFLC PROGRAM PARTICIPANT

"The support was excellent and I would use the services again if needed."

MILITARY ONESOURCE PARTICIPANT

About this Report

The report should be of interest to policymakers and program leadership. Policymakers can use study findings as they make decisions about continuation and expansion of nonmedical counseling provided through MFLC and Military OneSource. Program leadership can determine where the program is most effective and for whom, and can use the findings to pinpoint program areas in need of improvement or greater attention. This research was sponsored by ODASD (MC&FP) and conducted within the Forces and Resources Policy Center of RAND NDRI, a federally funded research and development center sponsored by the Office of the Secretary of Defense, the Joint Staff, the Unified Combatant Commands, the Navy, the Marine Corps, the defense agencies, and the defense Intelligence Community. For more information on the RAND Forces and Resources Policy Center, see http://www.rand.org/nsrd/ndri/centers/frp.html or contact the director (contact information is provided on the web page).

Acknowledgments

The study team is grateful for the support, oversight, and guidance provided by staff at the Office of Deputy Assistant Secretary of Defense for Military Community and Family Policy. In particular, Lee Kelley and our project monitor, Cathy Flynn.

We acknowledge the contributions of the MFLC counselors who provided feedback on the study procedures and who recruited participants for the study. We also thank the triage consultants at Military OneSource for their help recruiting participants for the study.

At RAND NDRI, we would like to thank the members of our research team, John Daly, Roald Euller, Ann Haas, Clarissa Sellers, Lemenuel Dungey, and Kendra Wilsher for their help with the project.

This publication benefited greatly from the assistance of Dori Walker, who designed the graphics and layout.

We also extend our thanks to Craig Bond, Kristie Gore, and John Winkler for their helpful reviews and feedback on this publication.
